IMAGES OF WAR

WAFFEN-SS AT ARNHEM SEPTEMBER 1944

RARE PHOTOGRAPHS FROM WARTIME ARCHIVES

Ian Baxter

Pen & Sword
MILITARY

First published in Great Britain in 2022 by
PEN & SWORD MILITARY
an imprint of Pen & Sword Books Ltd
Yorkshire – Philadelphia

ISBN 978-1-39901-294-2

A CIP catalogue record for this book is available from the British Library.

Typeset by Concept, Huddersfield, West Yorkshire, HD4 5JL.
Printed and bound in England by CPI Group (UK) Ltd, Croydon CR0 4YY.

MIX
Paper from responsible sources
FSC® C013604

Pen & Sword Books Limited incorporates the imprints of Atlas, Archaeology, Aviation, Discovery, Family History, Fiction, History, Maritime, Military, Military Classics, Politics, Select, Transport, True Crime, Air World, Frontline Publishing, Leo Cooper, Remember When, Seaforth Publishing, The Praetorian Press, Wharncliffe Local History, Wharncliffe Transport, Wharncliffe True Crime and White Owl.

For a complete list of Pen & Sword titles please contact
PEN & SWORD BOOKS LTD
47 Church Street, Barnsley, South Yorkshire, S70 2AS, England
E-mail: enquiries@pen-and-sword.co.uk
Website: www.pen-and-sword.co.uk
or
PEN & SWORD BOOKS
1950 Lawrence Rd, Havertown, PA 19083, USA
E-mail: uspen-and-sword@casematepublishers.com
Website: www.penandswordbooks.com

Contents

About the Author

Ian Baxter is a military historian who specialises in German twentieth-century military history. He has written more than fifty books including *Poland – The Eighteen Day Victory March, Panzers In North Africa, The Ardennes Offensive, The Western Campaign, The 12th SS Panzer-Division Hitlerjugend, The Waffen-SS on the Western Front, The Waffen-SS on the Eastern Front, The Red Army at Stalingrad, Elite German Forces of World War II, Armoured Warfare, German Tanks of War, Blitzkrieg, Panzer-Divisions at War, Hitler's Panzers, German Armoured Vehicles of World War Two, Last Two Years of the Waffen-SS at War, German Soldier Uniforms and Insignia, German Guns of the Third Reich, Defeat to Retreat: The Last Years of the German Army At War 1943–45, Operation Bagration – the Destruction of Army Group Centre, German Guns of the Third Reich, Rommel and the Afrika Korps, U-Boat War*, and most recently *The Sixth Army and the Road to Stalingrad*. He has written over a hundred articles including 'Last days of Hitler', 'Wolf's Lair', 'The Story of the V1 and V2 Rocket Programme', 'Secret Aircraft of World War Two', 'Rommel at Tobruk', 'Hitler's War With his Generals', 'Secret British Plans to Assassinate Hitler', 'The SS at Arnhem', 'Hitlerjugend', 'Battle of Caen 1944', 'Gebirgsjäger at War', 'Panzer Crews', 'Hitlerjugend Guerrillas', 'Last Battles in the East', 'The Battle of Berlin', and many more. He has also reviewed numerous military studies for publication, supplied thousands of photographs and important documents to various publishers and film production companies worldwide, and lectures to various schools, colleges and universities throughout the United Kingdom and the Republic of Ireland.

Introduction

The Arnhem landings are regarded as a great feat of arms, courage and tenacity as demonstrated by British paratroopers in a desperate last-stand situation. As this book describes, the paratroopers who landed in the Arnhem area on 17 September 1944 had no idea that two SS Panzer Divisions, the 9th and 10th, were recuperating and concealed in woods. A bloody battle followed.

Here, with text and photographs, some rare and unpublished, the reader will learn about the background of the *Hohenstaufen* and *Frundsberg* divisions, and that despite the war being only months from its end, the SS soldier was far from beaten and as determined as ever to hold on to as much of Europe as possible. This book captures the drama of that epic battle, showing how both sides fought desperately for a bridge over the Rhine.

SS-Obergruppenführer Wilhelm Bittrich. He became commander of the 9th SS Panzer Division *Hohenstaufen* in February 1943 until the end of June 1944. On 1 July 1944, he was appointed the commander of II SS Panzer Korps where he directed operations of his units in Normandy. In early September 1944, his Korps was instructed to relocate to the Arnhem area in Holland in order to rest its units.

(**Opposite, above**) Panzergrenadiers belonging to the 9th SS Panzer Division *Hohenstaufen* while on a march on the Eastern Front. The division took part in the relief of German forces trapped in what was known as the Kamenets-Podolsky Pocket in late March 1944.

(**Opposite, below**) A Volkswagen *Schwimmwagen* four-wheeled-drive amphibious car belonging to the 9th SS *Hohenstaufen*. The vehicle can be seen halted in the snow in 1944 next to a column of 15cm *Hummels* on special flatbed rail cars, all destined for the front lines in Russia.

(**Above**) A *Hummel* attached to the 9th SS *Hohenstaufen* in the winter of 1944 can be seen here in the snow. This vehicle's gun had been adapted and mounted on the *Geschützwagen* III/IV chassis and armed with a 15cm howitzer. This *Panzerfeldhaubitze* 18M *auf Geschützwagen* III/IV (Sf) *Hummel*, Sd.Kfz.165 entered service in 1943. Initially, designers had wanted to mount a 10.5cm le.FH.18 howitzer on the chassis of a Pz.Kpfw.III, but it was rejected in favour of the more powerful and larger Pz.Kpfw.IV chassis.

A FlaK crew from the 9th SS *Hohenstaufen* preparing for a fire mission in late March 1944. Units of this division were embroiled in the Battle of the Kamenets-Podolsky Pocket (or Hube Pocket), which was a Soviet plan to envelop the Wehrmacht's 1st Panzer Army of Army Group South. The envelopment occurred in late March 1944 during the Dnieper-Carpathian offensive and was the largest and most important operation of that offensive.

The first of two photographs showing units of the 10th SS *Frundsberg* Division during operations in the Ukraine in the early spring of 1944. The division's first battles were seen in Tarnopol, but it was then shifted to assist in the relief operation of the Kamenets-Podolsky Pocket.

An Sd.Kfz.250/1 belonging to the 10th SS *Frundsberg* during operations on the Eastern Front in April 1944.

(**Left**) *SS-Gruppenführer* Karl Fischer von Treuenfeld, commander of the 10th SS *Frundsberg* between November 1943 and late April 1944. (**Right**) *SS-Brigadeführer* Heinz Harmel became commander of the 10th SS *Frundsberg* in late April 1944 until the end of the war. He wears the Knight's Cross of the Iron Cross with Oak Leaves, with which he was decorated on 7 September 1943.

A *Sturmgeschutz* III advancing in the snow during operations in March 1944 in the Kamenets-Podolsky Pocket.

During operations on the Eastern Front and soldiers of the 9th SS cheer when one of their comrades raises a wicker container which more than likely contains alcohol.

The first of five photographs showing Panthers belonging to the II SS Panzer Korps while operating on the Eastern Front in March 1944. In late March/early April 1944, this Korps, alongside other reinforcements, was sent from France to the Eastern Front where it played the main role in deblockading the encircled 1st Panzer Army in the Kamenets-Podolsky Pocket. It was the first major transfer of forces from France to the East since the Führer Directive 51, which outlined that no transfers of any forces were allowed from the West to the East. After rescuing the better part of the 1st Panzer Army along with the 9th and 10th SS, the Korps then participated in the attempt to deblockade the trapped German garrison of the 4th Panzer Army in the town of Tarnopol.

611

612

612

(**Left**) *SS-Obergruppenführer* Paul Hauser, commander of the II SS Panzer Korps from June 1942 until the end of June 1944. (**Centre**) A photo taken of *SS-Brigadeführer* Sylvester Stadler during a command on the Eastern Front. Stadler was given command of the 9th SS from 10 July until he was relieved on 31 July 1944, only having held the position for three weeks. Ironically, he was then again given command of the division in October of that year until the end of the war. (**Right**) *SS-Oberführer* Friedrich Wilhelm Bock who took command of the 9th SS for only one month from the end of July until the end of August 1944.

A unit on the march belonging to the Panzer divisions of the II SS-Panzer corps – *Hohenstaufen* and *Frundsberg*. Following heavy fighting on the Eastern Front and then in Normandy, these divisions would be seen recouping in Holland in September 1944.

Panthers from the II SS Panzer Korps resting in a Norman village in July 1944.

A Pz.Kpfw.IV belonging to the 9th SS during operations in France in the summer of 1944. The *Hohenstaufen* suffered heavy losses from Allied fighter-bombers during its move to Normandy, delaying its arrival until 26 June 1944.

(**Opposite, above**) A stationary Panther from the 9th SS in Normandy in late June 1944. Almost half the division's tanks broke down during its drive to Normandy. When it arrived, the division's armoured units were reinforced by the newly-attached 102nd SS Heavy Panzer Battalion. This would provide *Hohenstaufen* with 127 additional combat vehicles including 79 Panther tanks.

(**Opposite, below**) Inside a wooded area and a column of Panthers from the II SS Panzer Korps is led by an Ausf.A, which has the full front mudflap extensions. The second Panther appears to be an Ausf.G variant.

(**Above**) Stationary Panthers inside some woods, more than likely from the II SS Panzer Korps resting during daylight hours.

Civilians pass a knocked-out *Jagdpanzer* IV in France in August 1944. By this time the Battle of Normandy was over and the German forces were in full retreat through France. Both the 9th and 10th SS had fought a number of rearguard actions during the retreat through France and Belgium, and in early September 1944 the exhausted formations were pulled out of the line for rest and refit near the Dutch city of Arnhem.

Deployment on the Eastern and Western Fronts up to Summer 1944

The SS Division *Hohenstaufen* was formed in France in February 1943, along with its sister formation the 10th SS Division *Frundsberg*. Initially *Hohenstaufen* was designated as a Panzergrenadier division, but by October 1943 it was upgraded to Panzer division status.

Command of the *Hohenstaufen* Division fell to *SS-Brigadeführer* Wilhelm 'Willi' Bittrich. *SS-Standartenführer* Lothar Debes was the first commander of the *Frundsberg* Division.

Most of the personnel in both divisions were either conscripted or volunteered. Some were transferred from other units, both from the Reich and *Volksdeutsche*, between the ages of 17 and 20. Most were older, seasoned soldiers who had gained combat experience on both the Eastern and Western fronts. They knew what to expect and offered the younger men a wealth of experience and knowledge. Many had already been members of the *Hitlerjugend*, and some had even served in *Sturmabteilung* (SA) or storm troops in the thirties.

Both the *Hohenstaufen* and *Frundsberg* had trained for nearly a year and were equipped to a high standard. They were regarded as crack SS units – the divisions had been built around a cadre of personnel from units such as *Leibstandarte* and *Das Reich*. Yet, when they had completed their training by early 1944, the situation for the German war machine was looking dire.

On the Eastern Front the war had deteriorated, and following the encirclement of the 1st Panzer Army in the Kamenets-Podolsky pocket in the Ukraine, Field Marshal Erich von Manstein urgently requested that the new fresh *Hohenstaufen* and *Frundsberg* divisions be sent to attempt to link up with the encircled force.

It had already been common practice, especially on the Eastern Front, for elite combat formations of the Waffen-SS to be rushed from one danger spot to another, sometimes with only the briefest of rest for refitting. These divisions had become known as the 'fire brigade' of the Third Reich. Wherever they were committed to battle, they were expected to attack. Sometimes the outcome was successful, but there were many times when they failed. Yet whatever the outcome, the result was always to delay the enemy advance. This had become the primary value of the Waffen-SS in the last two years of the war.

While *Hohenstaufen* and *Frundsberg* boarded the long trains bound for southern Russia, von Manstein's forces were being slowly bled to death inside the Kamenets-Podolsky Pocket. Tons of ammunition and fuel were being airlifted into the pocket so he did not have to abandon his heavy equipment and armour when the time came to break out. When the two new SS divisions arrived in southern Russia they launched a flank attack supported by the II SS Panzer Corps.

The II SS Panzer Corps was formed from the SS Division *Leibstandarte*, SS Division *Das Reich* and SS Division *Totenkopf*. Here on the Eastern Front it played the main role in unblockading the encircled 1st Panzer Army. Together with *Hohenstaufen* and *Frundsberg* they smashed into the tip of the Russian spearhead and allowed the trapped 1st Panzer Army to escape slaughter. As the panzers fought their way out towards the west, the entire SS force joined arms and counter-attacked to take the pressure off the retreating tanks. It seemed that the Waffen-SS had averted another Stalingrad.

After that, *Hohenstaufen* and *Frundsberg* were withdrawn to Poland to prevent a renewal of the Red Army advance, but Hitler stipulated that these divisions would be called upon if there was an Allied invasion of Western Europe.

By the summer of 1944 the Waffen-SS were fully aware that the Red Army had only been delayed, not halted. As both the southern and northern fronts withdrew and tried their best to stabilize their precarious defences against a growing enemy force, news had reached them that the Allies *had* landed in Western Europe. Hitler looked to the Waffen-SS divisions to save the situation.

Hohenstaufen and *Frundsberg* were sent to northern France along with the II Panzer Corps on 12 June 1944 to defend the city of Caen in Normandy. The *Hohenstaufen* Division's journey to France was hindered by heavy Allied fighter attacks, delaying its arrival until 26 June. Losses for the division were high, and almost half its tanks broke down during the move to Normandy. When the division arrived, its armoured force was reinforced by the newly-attached 102nd SS Heavy Panzer Battalion. This would provide *Hohenstaufen* with 127 additional combat vehicles including 79 Panther tanks. Its intended plan when it arrived in Normandy was to attack towards the Allied beachhead and prevent the British offensive to take Caen. The II SS Panzer Corps was instead put into the line to support the weakened forces defending Caen.

In the weeks that followed these SS formations, together with the 12th SS Panzer Division *Hitlerjugend*, *Lehr* Division and the 21st Panzer carried on resisting and fighting doggedly in and around Caen, which was slowly reduced to rubble. The fighting raged day and night. In the lanes and farm tracks that crisscrossed the Normandy countryside, rows of dead from both sides lay amid a mass of smashed and burned-out vehicles.

Hohenstaufen suffered almost 2,000 casualties, and as a result on 10 July the division was pulled back into reserve to be replaced by the 277th Infantry Division. The division's depleted Panzergrenadier regiments were eventually merged to form Panzergrenadier Regiment *Hohenstaufen*.

Despite the growing losses in the Normandy sector, the Waffen-SS divisions continued desperately trying to keep the Allies in check. The conditions of the Norman countryside favoured the SS grenadiers. Clusters of trees, tall hedges, ditches and lack of roads frustrated the Allied armoured units seeking to destroy enemy tanks in open areas. Because of this the SS were able to defend positions longer than the Allies had expected and inflicted huge casualties. However, savage Allied air attacks and naval bombardments gradually began to grind down the German defences. Movement was almost impossible by day, as any vehicles seen were immediately attacked and destroyed.

At the end of the first week of August, all regular and Waffen-SS divisions were fighting for survival. Corps and divisions remained in action on paper, but were shrinking to battalion size.

Calamity now threatened as the Americans broke out and the Normandy campaign became mobile. To save the German forces in Normandy from being completely encircled and destroyed, a series of rapid withdrawals were undertaken through the Falaise-Argentan gap. *Hohenstaufen* and *Frundsberg* just managed to avoid encirclement in the 'Falaise Pocket' along with the II Panzer Korps.

By 21 August the Battle of Normandy was over and the German forces were in full retreat. *Hohenstaufen* was down to approximately 7,000 men from 15,900 at the end of June. *Frundsberg* had lost all its tanks and artillery. Their only saviour from complete destruction as they withdrew across France into Belgium had been the support of II Panzer Corps.

In early September 1944 the then exhausted formations were pulled out of the line for rest and refit. *Hohenstaufen* and *Frundsberg* were withdrawn to lick their wounds in a quiet backwater in Holland: a town called Arnhem.

Assessment of the German Situation in Holland, September 1944

Defensive operations for the German soldier on the Western Front were very gloomy following their withdrawal from Normandy and then across France. They had fought desperately to maintain cohesion and hold their meagre positions that often saw thousands perish. By August 1944 the German forces were holding a battle line that had been severely weakened by the overwhelming strength of the Allies. To make matters worse, by this point in the war troop units were no longer being refitted with replacements to compensate for the large losses sustained. Supplies of equipment and ammunition were so insufficient in some areas of the front that commanders were compelled to issue their men with rations. As a consequence many soldiers had become increasingly aware that they were in the final stages of the war, and this included battle-hardened combatants. They had also realized that they were now fighting an enemy that was far superior to them.

Despite the adverse situation in which the German soldier was placed in the late summer of 1944, he was still strong and determined to fight with courage and skill. However, the German soldier had expended considerable combat efforts while lacking sufficient reconnaissance and the necessary support of tanks and heavy weapons to ensure any type of success. The Allies had constantly outgunned them, and the Luftwaffe air support was almost non-existent. The short summer nights had also caused considerable problems for the men, for they only had a few hours of darkness in which to conceal their night marches and construction of field fortifications. Consequently, the front-line soldier in the forward combat area was already continuously under fire from enemy artillery and aircraft. Ultimately, by this time the average German soldier was ill-prepared against any type of large-scale offensive. The infantry defensive positions relied upon sufficient infantry ammunition supply and the necessary support to ensure that they would able to hold their fortified areas. Without this, the German soldier was doomed. Commanders in the field were fully aware of the significant problems and the difficulties imposed by committing badly-equipped soldiers to defend the depleted lines of defence. However, in the end, they had no other choice than to order their troops to fight with whatever they had at their disposal.

By early September, Allied troops were now fighting in Belgium and were no more than 100 miles from its capital Brussels. Along the borders of Holland, Dutch civilians watched as thousands of dishevelled, exhausted German units shuffled along the roads. For hours a motley collection of military vehicles moved along the roads from the Belgian border into Holland. Both Wehrmacht and Waffen-SS troops used a variety of transport ranging from horses and cars to bicycles.

Although due to the spectacle in Holland it appeared that the German army was defeated, Hitler had already taken crucial measures to stem the German rout in Belgium and Holland. In order to close a gigantic hole between Antwerp and the area of Liege-Maastricht, soldiers were urgently rushed to the west to plug the hole by holding a line along the Albert Canal. With all possible speed, General Kurt Student, the 54-year-old founder of Germany's airborne forces, was ordered to organize a force which the Führer had redesignated as the '1st *Fallschirmjäger* Army' and rush them to Holland and Belgium. This time these elite paratroopers were to be used for ground operations. To bolster these troops, two divisions were planned for his new army. One was the 719th, which was made up of old inexperienced men stationed along the Dutch coast. The other was the 176th, which comprised semi-invalids and convalescents who had been organized together in separate battalions according to their various ailments. They even had special 'diet' kitchens for those suffering from various stomach disorders.

Other forces scattered across Holland comprised various ad hoc units including Luftwaffe troops, sailors and anti-aircraft crews, all of which were earmarked to strengthen Student's force. It would take at least five days for Student's entire force to reach the front, but his elite units were rushed onto special trains bound for Holland within twenty-four hours, all of which were to be unloaded and dug in along the Albert Canal as part of Walther Model's Army Group B.

By late afternoon of 5 September, Student's *Fallschirmjäger* were hastily digging in positions along the north side of the canal. In order to bolster its lines along the Albert Canal, Model deployed remnants of General Chill's 85th Infantry Division to strategic points on the northern bank of the river.

Other divisions that were also now located in Holland were none other than the II SS Panzer Korps. It had been fighting continuously from Normandy, and been ordered by Model to be disengaged from battle and relocated so that its commander, 50-year-old *SS-Obergruppenführer* Wilhelm Bittrich could be directed to supervise refitting and rehabilitation of the 9th SS *Hohenstaufen* and 10th SS *Frundsberg*. The site chosen for Bittrich was regarded as a peaceful sector where nothing was happening, at a point 75 miles behind the front. The area included the town of Arnhem.

Bittrich could not envisage the critical role that the 9th and 10th SS would play in the area. *Frundsberg* was assigned just north-east of Arnhem and was camouflaged in a densely-wooded national park. Nearby *Hohenstaufen* was encamped in woods, towns and villages of Doetinchem, Ruurlo, Zutphen, Apeldoorn and Beekbergen. Both of these SS formations were well within firing distance of Arnhem; some units no more than a couple of miles.

While resting these SS formations appeared to be in good spirits, despite the losses in France and the fact that many of the men knew the war was almost over. *SS-Obergefreiter* Wolfgang Dombrowski who was now attached to the engineer *Kampfgruppen Moeller* said that he believed the war was probably over, but most of the lower ranks were 18 to 19 years old and the officers 24 to 29. They were still youngsters and most were prepared to fight on. Alfred Ziegler who was attached to the SS *Panzerjäger Abteilung* 9 of the *Hohenstaufen* said that morale within the ranks was good and spirits were high. However, nothing was to prepare them for what was to happen in their rest area days later.

The *Frundsberg* cuff title.

The *Hohenstaufen* cuff title.

A well-camouflaged Pz.Kpfw.IV Ausf.H attached to the 10th SS *Frundsberg* during its retreat into Holland in early September 1944. On the evening of 4 September 1944, the division was ordered to establish a rearguard bridgehead west of Maastricht. Encountering no resistance, three days later *Kampfgruppe Harmel* reached its new assembly area.

A Panther attached to the 10th SS *Frundsberg* advancing along a Dutch road in early September 1944. On 7 September the divisional battle group drove through Venlo and Nijmegen to prepare its assembly areas north and east of Arnhem. Three days later on 10 September, *Frundsberg*'s sister division the *Hohenstaufen* was ordered to turn over its remaining operational vehicles to its sister unit. These included armoured vehicles, and two grenadier battalions and an artillery battalion were also transferred. This left the *Hohenstaufen* with only a cadre of approximately 2,500 men.

Six photographs showing Panther tanks attached to the 10th SS *Frundsberg*, which was part of the II SS Panzer Korps. The vehicles are being parked and concealed in a wooded area in order to avoid enemy aerial surveillance. These are some of the surviving vehicles from operations in France. Upon arriving in the Arnhem area, the majority of the remaining armoured vehicles would be loaded onto trains in preparation for transport to repair depots in Germany. Although the 9th and 10th SS were recuperating in the area of Arnhem, they were short of actual armour. The majority of their tanks that were available were older variants from training regiments. In fact, Arnhem was one of the last battles where the Pz.Kpfw.III Ausf.N variant from Panzer *Kompanie Mielke* was seen. The best-equipped unit was the 1st SS Panzer Regiment from the 10th SS Panzer Division *Frundsberg*. These were supplemented with a variety of Tiger 1s from various heavy tank battalions, Sd.Kfz.250 and 251 half-tracks (mostly equipped with heavy FlaK guns) and a *Hummel* under the command of Major Knaust, known as *Kampfgruppe Knaust*. As for the Panther, there were eight readily available, but these vehicles were highly vulnerable to infantry in urbanized combat. They were best suited to the flat open terrain of northern Holland where their very high-velocity 7.5cm guns could take out the highly vulnerable Sherman and Cromwell tanks.

Panzer crew belonging to the II SS Panzer Korps. These men are attached to the II.Abteilung, Pz.Reg.10, 6.Kompanie and pose for the camera prior to the Arnhem landings.

Three photographs showing Panther crews arriving in the Arnhem area. During operations in France the *Hohenstaufen* Division received 127 additional combat vehicles including 79 Panther tanks. Most of these vehicles were lost and the remaining units were quickly withdrawn into Holland and Belgium for rest, recuperation and to be sent back to the Reich for repair. Initially the plan for both the 9th and 10th SS was to replenish both divisions at the front to then form an Army Group reserve. Supplies to bolster the units were to be directly sent from the Reich. However, due to the severe losses in manpower, it was decided to move both divisions into the Arnhem area for recuperation and to increase their strength.

Three photographs taken in sequence showing a Panther crew making minor repairs to their vehicle while recuperating. Although both the *Frundsberg* and *Hohenstaufen* divisions had been defeated, they were not destroyed as a fighting unit. Their officers were able to maintain good order and discipline. Their retreat into Holland had not been a panic flight but an organized retreat. In fact, by the end of August 1944, as it continued its retreat westwards, the depleted *Hohenstaufen* formation actually fought a successful defensive action at Cambrai, destroying more than forty enemy tanks with some of its remaining Panthers. The division arrived in its new assembly area on 8 September near the city of Arnhem. From here the remaining units were expecting to reorganize and receive replacements and equipment. In fact, *Frundsberg* were expecting to receive Panther tanks, which was quite an achievement as many of the tanks in the area were under repair. There was only the Pz.Kpfw.IV *Abteilung* and a tank destroyer battalion readily available. Although *Jagdpanzer* IV assault guns had arrived, a number of them had already been dispatched to other areas of the front.

Two photographs of Panzer crewmen wearing their distinctive black Panzer uniforms. The crewman (17) wears the familiar special black Panzer uniform with M1938 black field cap, while the other crewman wears the later M1943 black field cap. These men were preparing for future operations and morale among both Panzer men and soldiers was good and they were in high spirits, in spite of the losses.

A Panther crewman manhandling two shells on his shoulders. He is wearing the denim Panzer working and summer vehicle uniform. These garments were considerably lighter and made life inside the baking hot compartment of the tank more bearable than the thick woollen black Panzer uniform.

Commanding officers and two Panther crew members converse in an open tract of land in the Arnhem area. By mid-September members of the *Hohenstaufen* were thinking about their families, 'as everything had virtually been packed for the move to Siegen'. Soon, so they thought, they would find themselves on trains back to their homeland while their vehicles were fixed and their units replenished with men and materials.

What appears to be a fresh-faced assault gun crew standing in front of two *Sturmgeschütz* III (StuG 40) Ausf.G vehicles, more than likely training. Both new assault gun and panzer crews were mostly untrained men who were not or only partially familiar with their vehicles but did not know how to handle tactical combat situations either. Note the StuG's StuK 40/L48 7.5cm gun barrels shielded by what appears to be metal sheeting. These vehicles would be used in the streets of Arnhem only days later. It would be the StuG Brigade 280 that sent seven StuG III Ausf.Gs and three StuH 42s to Arnhem.

A Pz.Kpfw.IV Ausf.H stationary in the Arnhem area in early September. Only two Pz.Kpfw.IVs (one Ausf.G and one Ausf.H) and six Pz.Kpfw.IIIs (Ausf.F, G, H and M) arrived in Arnhem. The other Panzers were probably either knocked out by Allied air attacks or had mechanical problems while on the train or travelling on the roads bound for Holland.

A number of shirtless SS grenadiers resting in the Arnhem area, probably in early September.

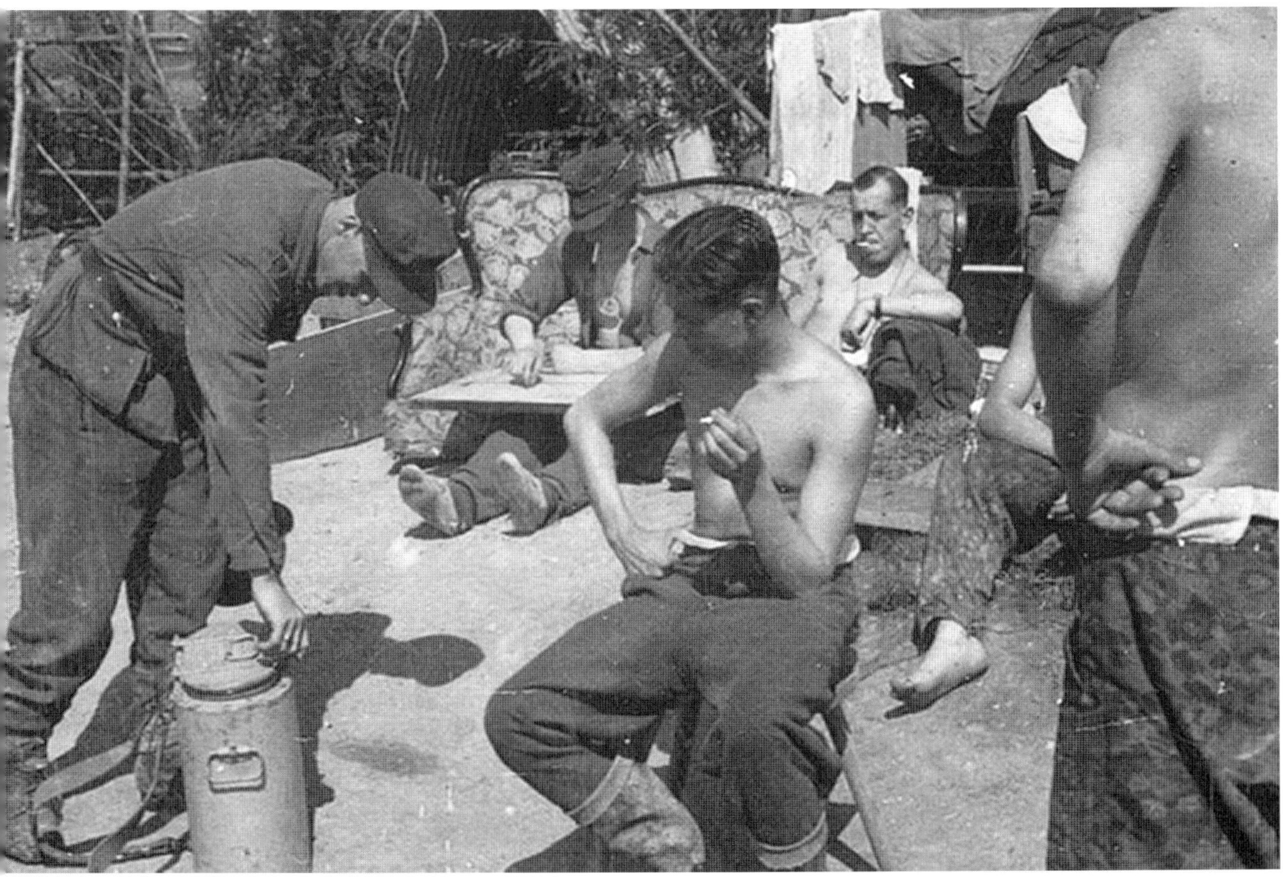

A Pz.Kpfw.IV crew poses for the camera while recuperating in southern Holland.

A Panther, more than likely part of the II SS Panzer Korps, advancing along a dirt track in southern Holland in early September.

Chapter One

The Landings

As the Allied armies thundered towards Germany in September 1944, Field Marshal Montgomery, ever eager to keep the retreating enemy on the run, had planned a massive airborne operation to seize the main river crossings in Holland stretching from Eindhoven to Arnhem, well ahead of an armoured thrust through the Dutch countryside and into the Reich. By dropping thousands of paratroopers behind enemy lines, he was convinced that these elite forces, the cream of the British army, could take the strategically-important bridge at Arnhem and then wrench open a corridor into the heartland of Germany, thus bringing an earlier end to the war. However, as Montgomery and his planners put the finishing touches to what was now called Operation MARKET GARDEN, they never realized that the intended drop-zone area would comprise elite Waffen-SS units recuperating.

During the morning of 17 September, Germany's airborne tactician, General Student, was at his headquarters in a cottage near Vught, about 16 miles west of Eindhoven, when he heard swarms of heavy bombers. From his desk he walked out onto the balcony and for some time watched the spectacle in the sky. Streams of aircraft – fighters, troop carriers and cargo planes – passed over. Some of them flew so low that Student and his chief of staff, Colonel Reinhard, ducked. Yet, in spite of this sight, Student was unconcerned by the nature of the airborne onslaught and returned to his paperwork. Throughout the morning there had been a heavy air attack and German units in the area did not regard this as particularly unusual. Bombers flying over to the Reich were a daily occurrence. Alfred Ziegler, a young dispatch rider serving in the 9th SS Anti-Tank Battalion of *Panzerjäger* 9, thought the sight of the mass of aircraft was truly amazing but no cause for concern. Even *SS-Obersturmbannführer* Walter Harzer, commander of the 9th SS, saw nothing regarding the aircraft to worry about. At his barracks at Hoenderloo, he was making his way over to the officers' mess for lunch when at that moment transport planes lumbered into sight. He never thought that the scene was the commencement of a massive airborne attack. Instead, he sat down quietly for something to eat with his officers and to toast the newly-decorated *SS-Haupsturmführer* Viktor Graebner. As Harzer ordered soup, outside many other soldiers began to focus on the strange phenomenon in the sky. Everyone seemed to become more captivated by the continual stream of aircraft. In the town of Deventer, which was a collection-point for Panzergrenadier Regiment 21 of the 10th SS, *SS-Rottenführer* Rudolf Trapp said that the sky was an armada, absolutely full of transports and bombers towing gliders.

SS-Standartenführer Lippert, who was commander of the SS NCO School *Arnheim*, soon realized that the hundreds of aircraft with escorts were coming down. He also observed through his binoculars that many of the planes had their doors open and large numbers of paratroopers were jumping out. *SS-Sturmbannführer* Klemeier, the commander of Training Battalion I/6, was hastily dispatched with a number of troops to investigate the reported landings around Nijmegen, Kraudenburg-Groesbeek and Mook. Nearby Sepp Krafft's SS Training and Replacement Battalion 16, which was the largest contained unit nearest to the landing-zone areas, was training in the Wolfheze woods and immediately he sent out patrols to investigate. It soon dawned on these units that this time the attack was different; it appeared to be an Allied airborne attack. *SS-Obergruppenführer* Bittrich received the first enemy reports by early afternoon and issued his first warning order. Both the 9th and 10th SS division headquarters were given a 'stand to' order. Within an hour a *Frundsberg* quick-reaction company was ordered to recce Arnhem and Nijmegen, assemble and defeat the Allies in the landing zones west of Arnhem by Oosterbeek. Fearing that the strategically-important Arnhem bridge was under threat, his units secured the bridge. Soldiers of the *Hohenstaufen* Division were to occupy the Nijmegen bridge and form a bridgehead to the south. Already all the spans of both Arnhem and Nijmegen bridges were prepared for demolition and protected by well-armed SS engineer parties and security detachments. A bridge commander was then assigned to each bridge and was given strict orders to blow them if they came under attack. From reports, it dawned on Bittrich that the airborne troops were going to seize the bridges before they were destroyed.

Over a period of just one hour a total of 331 British aircraft with 319 gliders and 1,150 American planes towing 106 gliders had begun landing men and equipment over three zones between Eindhoven and Arnhem. By this time, almost 20,000 parachute- and glider-borne infantry had been landed behind enemy lines. At the divisional headquarters of the 9th and 10th SS there was panic and bewilderment. Slowly, command and staff procedures began to function. Radio messages between the commands and units become more frequent and fluid, bringing a clearer picture of the situation. At Model's headquarters, however, there was still total confusion. Nobody understood what had happened, but they found themselves based almost in the British landing zones. Nearby, from his hotel headquarters, Sepp Krafft could see the surrounding heath jammed with gliders and troops, some only a few hundred yards away. He watched as enemy infantry assembled and began moving off to fight. He was now certain that these landings were part of a larger invasion force to seize the area on the Lower Rhine bridge at Arnhem.

Two photographs showing General Field Marshal Walther Mode, commander of Army Group B West. Many of the commanders in the field on the Western Front including the soldiers looked upon Model as the Führer's troubleshooter. He had been the commander that had first introduced in early 1944 the 'Shield and Sword' policy on the Eastern Front, which stated that retreats were intolerable unless they paved the way for a later counterstroke. Out on the battlefield Model was not only energetic, courageous and innovative, but was friendly and popular with his enlisted men. After the fighting in Normandy, Model established his headquarters at Oosterbeek near Arnhem, where he set about rebuilding Army Group B, which had almost been completely decimated on the Western Front. On 17 August 1944, Model was appointed to the temporary command of OB West.

(**Above**) *SS-Obersturmbannführer* Walter Harzer confers with one of his commanders. Harzer was commander of the *Hohenstaufen* Division. It was Harzer who at his barracks at Hoenderloo was making his way over to the officers' mess for lunch when he witnessed hundreds of transport planes come into sight. Initially, he never thought that the scene was the commencement of a massive Allied airborne attack.

(**Opposite**) The first of four photographs showing the huge Allied airborne landings in the Arnhem area on 17 September 1944, known as Operation MARKET GARDEN. Over a period of just one hour a total of 331 British aircraft with 319 gliders and 1,150 American planes towing 106 gliders had begun landing men and equipment over three zones between Eindhoven and Arnhem. Almost 20,000 parachute- and glider-borne infantry had been landed behind enemy lines. *(IWM)*

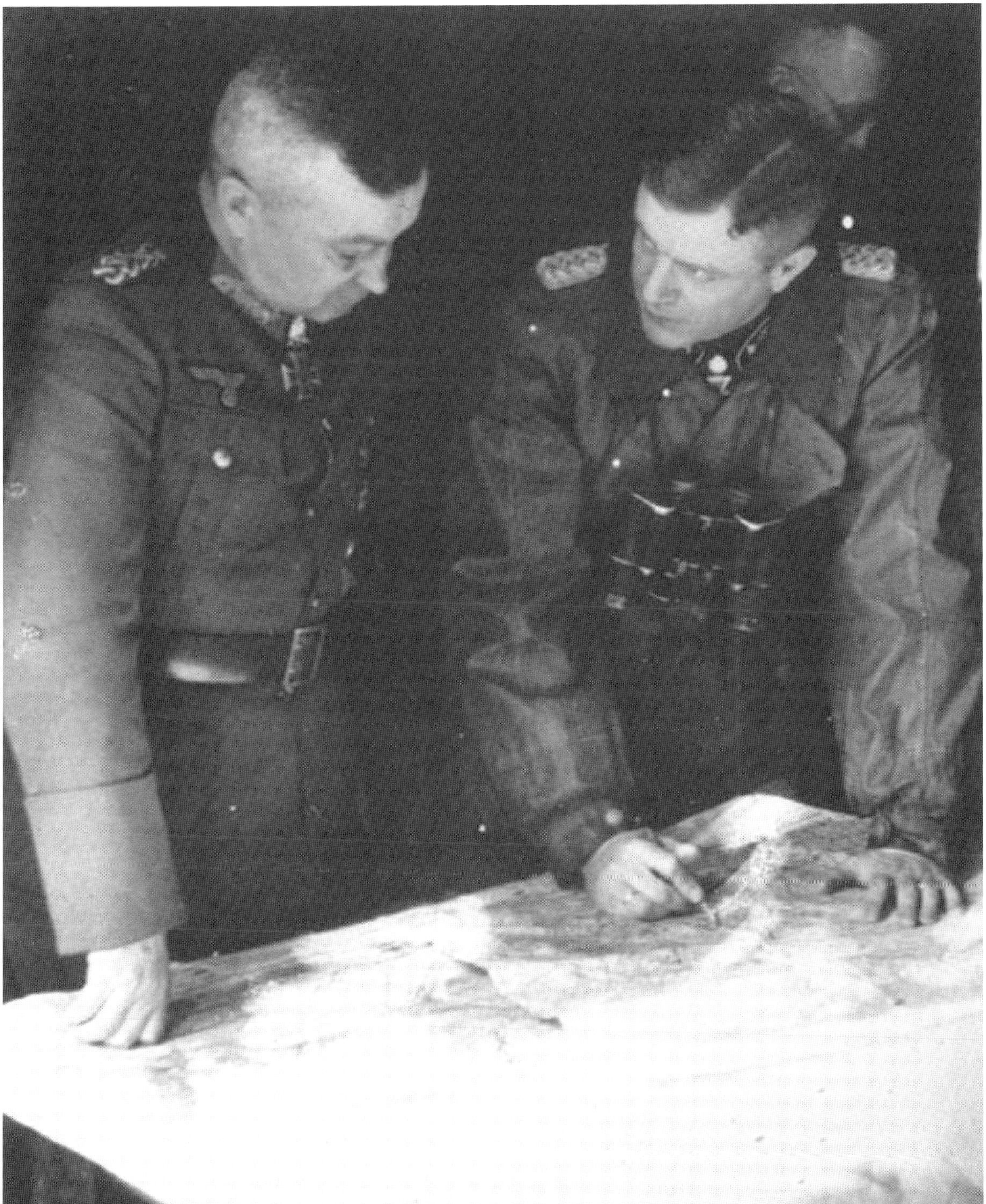

General Walther Model and *SS-Standartenführer* Heinz Harmel, commander of the 10th SS *Frundsberg* Division, confer with the aid of maps about the situation in the Arnhem area. This photograph was taken at Bittrich's headquarters where they discussed the landings and formulated a plan to blunt the Allied attack. (*BA/Halfen*)

(**Above**) From left to right of the photograph are Model, Bittrich, Knaust and Harmel. During mid-afternoon on 17 September Field Marshal Model arrived at Bittrich's headquarters to discuss the developing situation. (*BA/Halfen*)

(**Opposite**) Two photographs taken in sequence showing an SS grenadier armed with his MG 42 at the ready on board an Sd.Kfz.251/3. The vehicle passes along a road in the landing-zone area outside Arnhem on the road near Oosterbeek. Note a discarded parachute draped over a bush at the side of the road. This vehicle was attached to *Kampfgruppe Spindler*. (*BA/Halfen*)

(**Right**) An SS soldier surveys the sky for enemy aircraft using a Zeiss 12 × 60 Luftwaffe FlaK range-finder.

72 03

Troops belonging to the 176th Infantry Division dug in along the hedgerows in preparation to blunt the Allied advance following their landings in the area.

Wehrmacht troops supporting the SS advance towards Arnhem. Here soldiers pause in their march along a road.

Panzer crewmen during their march in the Arnhem area halted along a road with their well-camouflaged *Sturmgeschütz* III.

Under the supervision of their commanding officer newly-recruited FlaK gunners can be seen preparing their 2cm FlaK 30 weapon for a fire mission against aerial targets. A number of Allied aircraft were shot down over the Arnhem landing zone by FlaK guns. Because the Allied landing zones at Nijmegen and Arnhem were only a few miles from the Reich borders, other air defence units were also quickly alerted and employed.

(**Above**) A group of Waffen-SS Panzergrenadiers and a Panzer crewman during a pause in their march towards Nijmegen. When the Allied airborne assault was launched on 17 September 1944, they were immediately met by strong German resistance. While the American 82nd and 101st Airborne divisions had quickly consolidated their positions, taking the bridge town of Eindhoven and reaching Nijmegen, they soon began faltering against unexpectedly heavy German resistance that was rushed to the area. At Arnhem the situation was even worse, with Allied troops finding themselves entangled in thick relentless fighting against tough well-seasoned Waffen-SS Panzer troops. To make matters worse, there were other elite German forces in the area also supporting the main Panzer divisions including *SS-Unterführerschule Kampfgruppen* and some 400 troops from the 16th *SS-Stammbataillon*, and a number of Dutch SS police, Wehrmacht and Luftwaffe ground troops.

(**Opposite, above left**) *Fallschirmjäger truppen* advancing along a Dutch lane. These soldiers are part of the 1st Battalion of *Fallschirmjäger* Regiment 2, which had been a hastily-formed unit. Their combat effectiveness was regarded as low and had not developed cohesion. Most of the regiment was made up of recruits that had little training, with many of them not even having held a rifle before. Nevertheless, the regiment was committed to *Kampfgruppe Walther*, where these soldiers were given light anti-tank weapons mainly comprising *Panzerfausts* and were put in line to stem Allied armour.

(**Opposite, above right**) An interesting photograph showing an antiquated PaK 35/36 anti-tank gun being hitched to a captured American jeep. This PaK gun is attached to SS Battalion *Krafft* Company. This is one of two that belonged to this unit. (*BA/Halfen*)

(**Opposite, below**) A *Sturmgeschütz* III Ausf.G from Panzer Brigade 107 on the move. This brigade was employed as a quick reactionary unit against lightly-armed paratroopers that had just landed. The airborne troops did not stand a chance against its firepower.

SS-Standartenführer Heinz Harmel, commander of the 10th SS pictured on the left, was a 38-year-old veteran who was liked by his men. Harmel had reached his new assembly area on 7 September.

A heavy *Fallschirmjäger* MG 42 machine-gun crew dug in between Nijmegen and Arnhem. The Germans soon identified the key objectives of the Allied offensive and immediately ordered units to dig in along positions where they could disrupt or thwart the enemy's advance.

SS riflemen can be seen let loose firing wildly with their Karabiner 98k bolt-action rifles into the sky as enemy paratroopers begin landing in the Arnhem area. Machine guns and anti-tank guns were also brought to bear on the paratroopers. Many of the Paras were shocked at the resistance after being told that there would be minimal opposition.

SS-Hauptsturmführer Dr Egon Skalka, who was senior doctor in the 9th SS *Hohenstaufen*. It was Skalka who would later negotiate the evacuation of British wounded out of Arnhem.

Motorcyclists pause in their march in southern Holland. While one motorcyclist smokes a cigarette, his comrade reads a newspaper.

An SS officer converses with members of the *Fallschirmjäger* during their march along a road to meet the developing threat in the Arnhem area.

A young SS soldier wearing his summer camouflage smock and matching trousers on the side of a road. He is armed with the standard infantry issue Karabiner 98k bolt-action rifle.

Chapter Two

First Attacks

As the Allied airborne attack unfolded, Sepp Krafft's Panzergrenadier Training Reserve Battalion knew it was tasked to prevent the movement of British forces in the area and stop them reaching the Arnhem bridge. Hurriedly his companies were positioned along the Wolfheze road almost bordering Renkum Heath. Machine-gun platoons dug in and held each end of the line while the remainder were scattered in the surrounding woods and undergrowth.

As Krafft frantically issued orders and directed his men for attack, a staff car sped up to his headquarters and General Kussin hurried inside to observe first-hand what was happening. Looking across the heath, Kussin was able to observe the vast British air-drop. Gliders were still landing and he could clearly hear heavy machine guns engaging them as they came into land. From all over Krafft's positions, British paratroopers and SS became embroiled in heavy fighting. Supported by mortars and anti-tank guns on the main approaches, heavy forest skirmishes raged all afternoon against the British 1st and 3rd battalions of the Parachute Regiment. Along the edges of the Wolfheze road, the smell of burning pine trees wafted across the German positions as areas of the heath were set ablaze. Fighting in parts of the heath was intense and the British paratroopers were surprised by the strong resistance in the area. They had been under the impression that German defences in the area would have been minimal and had not expected such strong fighting and this from Waffen-SS units. Yet, despite the heavy resistance, the British 1st Air Landing Brigade, commanded by Brigadier Hicks, continued to fight doggedly to try to secure the drop zones around Wolfheze. In their distinctive camouflage battle smocks and crash helmets, laden with guns and ammunition, Brigadier Lathbury's 1st Parachute Brigade had been ordered to capture the main road and pontoon bridges in Arnhem. It was not until late afternoon/early evening that 1 and 3 Para had managed to claw their way past Krafft's positions. By that time, some British company groups had made their way into the western suburbs of Arnhem itself. For 1 and 3 Para, the drive on Arnhem was far from over. They were constantly engaged in bitter skirmishes. Hardened but desperate Waffen-SS troops, inferior in strength but supplemented by tanks, half-tracks and artillery, forced the Paras to fight a savage inch-by-inch battle of attrition. It seemed that everything now depended upon Colonel John Frost's 2 Para.

Frost's men had advanced more successfully. He had taken his battalion due south along the Lower Rhine road meeting little resistance. Frost's objective was the Arnhem bridge. *SS-Rottenführer* Rudolf Trapp's weak company of about fifty *Frundsberger* 1st SS were on bicycles pedalling from Deventer to Arnhem in order to meet the developing threat.

At Bittrich's headquarters at Doetinchem, Model arrived telling stories that he had barely escaped capture at the hands of the British parachutists while sitting down to lunch at the Hotel Tafelberg, but Model was not to be deterred. He was known by his men to be a man steady in adversity, and he immediately got down to business and directed the countermeasure against the Allies in the Arnhem and Nijmegen area. While II Panzer Korps was to attack and destroy the enemy at Nijmegen and Arnhem, General Student and the 1st *Fallschirmjäger* was given dual missions of stopping the British drive on the town. General Christiansen, the Armed Forces Commander Netherlands, was, in addition to the II Panzer Korps, to attack Arnhem. The force, under the command of General Hans von Tettau, known by his troops as *Division Tettau*, consisted of a collection of regional defence and training battalions that had been quickly thrown together as ad hoc units. Bittrich's II Panzer Korps was also to be further bolstered by a motorized infantry battalion commandeered from *Wehrkreis* VI and the re-routed 280th Assault Gun Brigade.

With the alarm now raised, companies of the 9th SS began to collect together. They arrived on horse-drawn carts, bicycles, on foot and literally anything else they could muster into service. Twenty trucks from *Hohenstaufen*'s transport resources shuttled companies through the centre of Arnhem towards the sound of gunfire in the western suburbs of the town. The newly-decorated *SS-Hauptsturmführer* Viktor Graebner was instructed to take his Reconnaissance Battalion to assess the strength of the Allied airborne troops between Arnhem and Nijmegen. By early evening, Graebner's column of SS armoured cars and half-tracks, totally fitted and cleared for action, reached the Arnhem bridge and thundered across. A mile past the southern end of the bridge, Graebner stopped his armoured car to report that there was still no sign of the enemy. He continued patrolling both sides of the road, and when his armoured column reached Nijmegen, his radio messages reported that there was no enemy. In fact, what Graebner did not know was that his battalion and forward elements of Frost's 2 Para had missed each other by approximately an hour.

Flakpanzer IVs of the 9th SS Panzer Division on a road in the Arnhem area. *(BA/Bender)*

An SS grenadier during his march to Arnhem.

Due to heavy enemy ground and aerial activity grenadiers are on the march towards Arnhem, half-concealing themselves along a ditch at the side of a road.

A group of 9.SS *Hohenstaufen* soldiers pose for the camera during operations in the Arnhem area.

A 9.SS assault gun crew can be seen next to a stationary halftrack. Note the dot 44 SS camouflage uniforms.

Two photographs showing *truppen* on bicycles bound for Arnhem. It was *SS-Rottenführer* Rudolf Trapp's weak company of about fifty *Frundsberger* 1st SS that bicycled from Deventer to Arnhem in order to meet the developing Allied threat.

Wehrmacht, Luftwaffe and Waffen-SS soldiers have hitched a lift on board lorries bound for Arnhem.

A *Sturmgeschütz* III belonging to Assault Gun Brigade 280 rumbles along a street coming into Arnhem from the north. Both Wehrmacht and Waffen-SS elements would support its drive. *(BA/Halfen)*

A group of Luftwaffe ground *truppen* pose for the camera next to a camouflaged *Sturmgeschütz* III Ausf.G before it resumes operations in the Arnhem area. The soldiers wear a variety of uniforms including *Fallschirmjäger*, assault gun crewman's field grey uniforms, jump smocks and tropical uniforms.

General Hans von Tettau, commander of *Kampfgruppen von Tettau* but known by his troops as *Division Tettau*. His *Kampfgruppen* comprised a collection of regional defence and training battalions that had been quickly thrown together as ad hoc units.

A *Fallschirmjäger* MG 42 heavy machine-gunner who has taken up a position on the outskirts of Arnhem in order to help prevent further Allied troops entering the town.

A light SS MG 34 team during a fire mission against any enemy target.

Two Allied aerial reconnaissance photographs showing the Arnhem bridge. Within twenty-four hours of the Allied landing, the spans of both Arnhem and Nijmegen bridges were prepared for demolition and protected by well-armed SS engineer parties and security detachments. A bridge commander was then assigned to each bridge and was given strict orders to blow them if they came under attack. *(IWM)*

On a road leading into the town of Arnhem and *Sturmgeschütz* III assault guns support grenadiers as they edge along while under fire.

PaK gunners during a fire mission against an Allied target. The Panzergrenadier Regiment *Frundsberg* had been ordered to form an anti-tank company of twelve guns within its own organization, four of which were to be motorized. All experienced gunners from other units were quickly drafted into the new company.

Chapter Three

Battle for Arnhem

Moving rapidly through the deserted streets of Arnhem, Frost's 2 Para were barely a mile from the great concrete and steel span bridge. His men were amazed by the sheer scale and size of the bridge. To some of them the high-arched girders spanning the Rhine looked intimidating. The concrete ramps alone were huge constructions with roads running beneath them along the river from west to east. On either side, the rooftops on the surrounding buildings came up to the level of the ramps. It had taken Frost and his men almost seven hours of fighting on the march to reach their main objective.

Behind 2 Para approaching Arnhem from the north-west, the 3rd Company of the *Frundsberg* Panzergrenadier Regiment 21 abandoned their bicycles on the outskirts of the town and made their way on foot towards the bridge. At first it was not apparent to Trapp's company that they were moving behind a British unit until they came across scattered articles of enemy equipment with dead British and German soldiers. Immediately, the SS troopers took evasive action and advanced along the street carefully, darting from one house to another. As they scurried beneath the level of the bridge searching for their enemy, the streets of Arnhem were suddenly brought to life by machine-gun fire and screams on the main span. Unknown to Trapp, up above, Frost's Paras were attempting to cross the bridge and had come under heavy machine-gun fire from the pillbox at the northern end. In an instant there was a huge succession of explosions as an ammunition hut was hit. The pillbox defending the bridge was also engulfed by flames as British PIAT rounds bored home, thundering into the bunker and burning alive the young SS soldiers inside. Simultaneously, Trapp's men came under heavy fire from all directions. Nobody knew for certain who was firing at who. As they dived for cover, it soon became apparent that the British had already begun taking up positions in the surrounding houses overlooking the bridge.

During the night, German vehicles from *SS-Hauptsturmführer* Karl Heinz Euling's 10th SS arrived at the northern end of the bridge, intent on crossing to Nijmegen. Unaware that the British were already firmly established and pointing their guns directly at them, Euling's leading company rumbled into view and was immediately exposed to a fierce fire-fight. In the short battle that followed, three lorries attempting to force a passage across the bridge exploded. The occupants bailed out, some in flames, and were killed in the crossfire. The burning wreckage now blocked the bridge, making it almost impossible to pass.

Stationed in a number of houses overlooking the bridge, Frost's men gazed across at the damage. Frost knew that just hours earlier he could have captured the bridge, but now, on the south bank, he was confronted by a group of angry and determined SS Panzergrenadiers, which appeared to be moving up and taking positions in order to remove and destroy the paratroopers.

SS-Standartenführer Heinz Harmel, who had just returned from Berlin, had expected to move his SS *Frundsbergers* across the bridge in order to meet the developing threat in Nijmegen where the 82nd Airborne Division had landed. Angry and frustrated, Harmel's entire division was to be re-routed and taken over the Rhine by ferry landing, some 8 miles south of Arnhem. He knew the cumbersome makeshift ferry crossing would be a slow, tedious way of reaching Nijmegen, and by ferrying all his armour and men, his units might not be in action for more than five days. As he stood and watched the columns of congested vehicles in the streets, Harmel knew there was only one solution to the problem. He would have to take the Arnhem bridge and open a route to Nijmegen.

During the remaining hours of darkness on the morning of 18 September, *SS-Sturmbannführer* Brinkmann's 10th SS *Kampfgruppe*, under command of the 9th SS, were given the task, along with the 25-year-old *SS-Sturmbannführer* Hans Peter Knaust's Panzergrenadier Training and Replacement Battalion *Bocholt*, of clearing the northern ramp of the British. As these forces got into position, pressure was still being maintained on the British west of the bridge. Parts of Panzergrenadier Regiment 21 could be clearly heard fighting as more British paratroopers tried desperately to punch a way through the streets of Arnhem to reach Frost at the bridge. For hours, house-to-house combat raged with the Germans even fighting a series of hand-to-hand duels. As houses caught fire, panicking civilians that had been taking shelter in their homes broke cover and rushed out into the streets, only to be mistakenly cut down.

Across the road from Frost's Paras, on a side street Captain Eric Mackay had managed to hold positions in two houses in the area and set up a command post in a school, despite the prospect of being overwhelmed and killed by the SS.

At first light, the stillness of the morning was broken by a number of demolition charges that were tossed through the windows by *Kampfgruppe* Brinkman's troopers. SS soldiers then began their first attack. First, attempts were made to infiltrate British positions from the east. As heavy machine-gun fire and mortars were brought to bear on Frost's and Mackay's positions, an SS attack was made on a number of occupied houses, resulting in heavy casualties among the assaulting troops. With these losses, the SS fired a *Panzerfaust* directly at a British-occupied house. The 20lb projectile crashed into the building, blowing out windows and debris. Through the screams of badly injured soldiers the Germans charged the house, lobbing grenades and shooting as they advanced over the rubble. A 21-year-old SS section commander, Alfred Ringsdorf, said that it was the hardest battle he had ever fought.

With the British still holding on fanatically and continuing to blunt a succession of heavy attacks, Brinkmann ordered a lorry assault against Frost's fortified houses. As the trucks came into view along Kade Strasse, the British opened up a barrage of fire that immediately blunted the vehicle attack. Those soldiers that managed to leap from their burning lorries were then cut down by British Bren guns.

Following the same route as the failed lorry infantry assault, a group of SS troopers hidden inside an ambulance also met a similar fate, being annihilated outside Frost's headquarters. Frustrated by the British defenders, Brinkmann's reconnaissance battalion then attempted an armoured rush. Beneath the bridge, the battalion of light tanks, half-tracks and armoured cars came up against a wall of fire. Two 6-pounder British anti-tank guns brought leading elements of the SS column to a flaming halt. The surviving troops were then shot and killed.

German commanders were now aware of the significant strength of their resilient foe. They could not hope at this stage that a combined tank and infantry assault could break through the warren of fortified houses protecting the bridge. It was now up to *SS-Hauptsturmführer* Viktor Eberhard Graebner, commander of Reconnaissance Battalion 9, who had returned just hours earlier from Nijmegen, to storm the bridge itself and recover it from the British.

A heavily-camouflaged convoy of stationary German vehicles outside Arnhem. Movement by day was perilous for German vehicles and most marches were undertaken at night or when it was considered safe to do so.

An SS *truppen* with his Karabiner 98k bolt-action rifle slung over his back and holding an ammunition box.

A young SS machine-gunner smiles for the camera. He wears an ammunition belt around his neck. His inexperience in the field is shown by the belt being carried incorrectly as most veteran machine-gunners wore their belts with the bullets pointing outwards so they would not cause injury or discomfort by digging into their body. Note his M1924 stick grenade stuck into his black leather infantryman's belt. He wears a pair of 6 × 30 Zeiss binoculars.

(**Above**) Troops hitch a lift on board a *Sturmgeschütz* III bound for the Arnhem area. This assault gun was part of the 9th SS and was attached to *Kampfgruppe* Walther.

(**Opposite, above**) SS troops can be seen walking along a road being supported by a StuG III.

(**Opposite, below**) Grenadiers supporting a camouflaged *Sturmgeschütz* III Ausf.G as it advances along a road. Note that no machine gun is mounted on the roof of this vehicle for local defence. For some reason it is missing. *(BA/Halfen)*

(**Opposite, above**) A view of the wreckage strewn across the Arnhem bridge.

(**Opposite, below**) A well-camouflaged late *Sturmgeschütz* variant rolls along a road with soldiers from the 9th SS surveying a row of houses for potential enemy hide-outs.

(**Above**) SS soldiers trying to deduce the location of their enemy. Close-quarter fighting was widespread in the streets of Arnhem with a number of hand-to-hand battles.

Panzergrenadiers of Assault Gun Brigade 280 move into the town of Arnhem ready to do battle with the enemy. The vehicle is a *Sturmhaubitz* 42G late-variant type. Earlier in the year in April 1944, 280 had been pulled out of the Eastern Front after being almost decimated near Tarnopol. The brigade was sent to Hadersleben in Germany for a refit and recuperation, and then to Denmark. In July it was dispatched to the North Sea coast in the area of Öchsbyl. Following the Allied airborne landing in the Arnhem area the battery was rushed to Holland, arriving on 19 September. In total there were seven StuG III Ausf.G variants and three StuH 42 types.

The first of five photographs showing Assault Gun Brigade 280 with supporting Panzergrenadiers during fighting inside Arnhem. The brigade was attached to *Kampfgruppe* Spindler, and for the battle it was employed singly or in pairs to various subsidiary *Kampfgruppen* depending upon their requirements. Its first operation on 19 September was established at the head of Utrechtstrasse, as the armoured vehicles gathered in the vicinity of the railway station waiting for the command to move forward. Its first encounter with the enemy was against the British 4th Parachute Brigade at the PGEM building just beyond the Municipal Museum.

SS-Hauptsturmführer Karl Heinz Euling of the 10th SS. It was Euling that led an attack across the northern end of the Arnhem bridge. However, Euling's leading company was immediately exposed to a fierce fire-fight and the attack across the bridge was blunted.

Captured British airborne soldiers and a Jeep being utilised probably by *truppen* belonging to the 9th SS *Hohenstaufen*.

An SS soldier takes a drink from his canteen.

A photograph taken from a halted *Sturmgeschütz* III shows a number of other assault guns advancing along a road. Note the Pkw.K1 *Kübelwagen* type 62 knocked out of action during heavy fighting on 18 September. A German soldier lies dead next to the vehicle. *(BA/Halfen)*

Youthful *Fallschirmjäger* soldiers are seen here moving along a road. Note the soldier armed with the *Panzerfaust*. Many of the troops of the *Fallschirmjäger*, especially those with limited battlefield experience and training, were issued with these anti-tank weapons as they were easy to use and required hardly any teaching.

A *Sturmgeschütz* III Ausf.G which has advanced from Oude Kraan and is advancing along Onoeriangs towards the junction with Utrechtseweg. Note the soldiers from the 9th SS walking among abandoned equipment left behind by British parachutists.

German troops inspect a destroyed British 6-pounder at Arnhem.

Two photographs taken in sequence showing SS soldiers climbing over railings in order to attack and drive out British troops. In a number of areas SS attacks were often thinly spread out but supported by Pz.Kpfw.IVs and *Sturmgeschütz* assault guns which gave them the added punch required to successfully flush out their resilient opponents.

(**Opposite, above**) A camouflaged *Sturmgeschütz* III from Assault Gun Brigade 280 moves along a street with houses showing the unmistakable signs of battle. A dead British paratrooper lies in the road next to the assault gun.

(**Opposite, below**) *Sturmgeschütz* III from Assault Gun Brigade 280 advancing along a road with SS troops in support. During the fighting in the Arnhem area the brigade lost at least two of its StuGs. One of these was lost in Benedendorpsweg and was attached to *Kampfgruppe* Harder. The other was destroyed in Ploegseweg as part of *Kampfgruppe* Von Allwörden.

(**Above**) During the heat of the battle and troops of a *Kampfgruppe* attached to the Korps Feldt fighting in the Groesbeck area.

Soldiers with their bicycles on the corner of a street during a lull in the fighting. Bullet holes have riddled a wall of a house, evidence of the heavy fighting that raged here. By this period of the war, especially in southern Holland, the lack of vehicles saw some units predominately mounted on bicycles. A number of units arrived in Arnhem on bicycles.

A *Sturmgeschütz* III Ausf.G heading along a road for Oosterbeek, which is littered with enemy equipment and dead paratroopers.

Chapter Four

Retaking Arnhem

Commander *SS-Hauptsturmführer* Viktor Eberhard Graebner had a mixture of various armoured vehicles consisting of twenty-two armoured cars, personnel carriers, half-tracks, some of which mounted the 7.5cm anti-tank gun, and even a few infantry trucks. His powerful armoured units represented the strongest concentration in the 9th SS. At 9.00am on 19 September, convinced that speed and the shock of heavy concentrated fire would protect them, the SS commander signalled the attack across the bridge to commence. Through the acrid haze of cordite smoke, the bridge began to vibrate as the rattling column surged forward. Completely exposed to hostile fire, Graebner urged his men forward into action. Gaining momentum, the vehicles raced over the summit of the bridge, expertly nosing around the wreckage of the previous attacks. The attack was so swift that leading elements of the column sped over the bridge unscathed, down the ramp and into the town centre. From the rooftops, windows and slit trenches, British paratroopers opened up with every weapon available and poured a storm of fire into the slower under-powered half-tracks. British sappers on the side of the ramp began taking out half-track drivers. Hand grenades were lobbed and mortars fired. Vehicles were brought to a flaming halt, their crew members abandoning the burning wreckage, only to be shot one by one. In the mayhem and confusion, half-tracks began colliding with each other and became entangled across the road. Vehicles coming up behind tried furiously to force a passage, frantic to gain the northern side. However, unable to advance any further, some surviving SS infantry, desperately seeking refuge from the slaughter, either crawled back across to the southern side of the bridge or, realizing their position was hopeless, leaped over the bridge's balustrades into the lower Rhine, preferring an uncertain death below to certain death above.

Graebner's attack proved to be a catastrophe. On the southern side his surviving troopers from Reconnaissance Battalion 9 were dazed and shocked by the ferocity of the British defence. Looking across the bridge, soldiers could see their dead comrades huddled by their burned-out vehicles where they had fallen. It soon became apparent that Graebner, an enigmatic figure to his men, had not come back. It was later discovered that he had been shot while directing his armoured column across the bridge. His dead body was to remain on the bridge until it could finally be recovered.

The death of Graebner and his failure to capture the bridge had a big impact on his men and those members of the *Hohenstaufen* divisional staff that had known him well. For them, the realization now began to emerge that capturing the bridge would be no easy task.

The burned-out wreckage of Graebner's futile and costly attack now blocked the road and prevented further attempts to reach Frost's fortified houses. As Knaust's *Kampfgruppe* relieved Euling's exhausted battalion, the main focal point of the battle for the bridge was shifted north.

Elsewhere, von Tettau's attacks on the landing zones west of Arnhem had made steady progress. For almost twenty-four hours, his SS troopers had run a gauntlet of heavy attacks in an attempt to encircle the British landing zones and appeared to have them in his grasp. However, as they began securing areas towards Oosterbeek, another Allied airborne attack appeared in the skies moving west. SS FlaK units immediately manned their guns and started firing at the approaching aircraft. Also from inside the surrounding woods and across the heathland vehicle groups of riflemen began shooting into the sky. Other soldiers balancing MG 42s on upturned wooden ammunition boxes fired burst after burst of fire at the approaching aircraft. Swarms of transport planes flew into view plus aircraft towing gliders. Soon planes were dropping thousands of paratroopers that were falling towards the drop zone south of the ED Arnhem road. A crescendo of machine-gun and FlaK fire burst into the air, hitting hundreds of bodies of Brigadier John 'Shan' Hackett's 4th Parachute Brigade. Many of the men were killed before they even reached the ground. The Paras had been told that Arnhem was lightly defended and the drop zones were now cleared. Yet as they approached the ground through waves of bullets, beneath their feet there was a full battle raging.

Hackett's newly-arrived 4th Parachute Brigade was to secure the high ground north of Arnhem, while the glider-borne 2nd South Staffordshire Battalion began to move into Arnhem in support of the advance, already being bitterly contested by the 1 and 3 Paras which had suffered considerable losses. Then 11 Para was to follow. Their main objective was to coordinate their joint thrusts in a vain attempt to reach the bridge. The British tried to charge through the streets of Arnhem, which was now known by the troops as the 'urban valley of death'. Assailed on three sides by heavy fire from *SS-Hauptsturmführer* Hans Moeller and *SS-Obersturmbannführer* Ludwig Spindler's *Kampfgruppen*, as well as remnants of the *Hohenstaufen* Reconnaissance Battalion, the British became more aggressive as the urban battle intensified. All over Arnhem savage and bloodthirsty battles were fought. The British closed in fast, and a number of terrifying hand-grenade duels developed. In the heat of the battle, soldiers occupied houses and gardens and fired at anything that moved. Columns of paratroopers were desperate to reach Frost at the bridge, but as they advanced along the streets they were killed by heavy SS fire. Slowly and systematically the Paras were ground down by the overwhelming strength of their foe. Almost all their NCOs and officers had either been killed or wounded. No. 1 Para had reached the old harbour and could see the towering bridge arching over the river. They were less than a mile from their objective, but this would be the nearest they would ever get to Frost. Even continued attacks by the 4th Parachute Brigade were unable to restore the catastrophic situation.

Throughout 19 September the survivors of the destroyed British battalions fled and made a contested withdrawal towards Oosterbeek and then on to Wolfheze, but still fighting a series of heavy battles against a growing and more resilient SS soldier.

Yet, in spite of the deteriorating situation for the British, Frost's beleaguered paratroopers were still holding several badly-damaged houses, but were now being constantly attacked by two *Kampfgruppen* – Brinkmann and Knaust – from three directions.

Tiger tanks were now used to force a passage through the wreckage of Graebner's failed attack. In support from the southern bank German 8.8cm FlaK guns were used to bombard Frost's positions. An SS Section Commander Alfred Ringsdorf remarked that the only way to get the British out 'was to carry them out feet first'. Grenadier Private Horst Weber said the FlaK bombardment was first directed against the rooftops of Frost's buildings. For hours the buildings were bombarded. Suffering acute shortages of supplies and ammunition plus mounting casualties, *SS-Standartenführer* Harmel ordered his staff to arrange a temporary truce with Frost. However, despite his precarious position, Frost would not negotiate with the Germans and told them to 'go to hell'. Harmel's attempt at a truce had failed. The battle once more began in all its fury.

Slowly and methodically Brinkmann and Knaust's *Kampfgruppe* moved in for the kill. Out of the eighteen battered buildings that 2 Para had initially occupied, Frost's men now only held ten of them. King Tiger tanks joined the fighting. These 60-ton monsters prowled through the rubble-strewn streets, pumping shell after shell into each house. Often, as the British darted out, its machine guns opened up, spraying the scrambling defenders in the back. All around 2 Para's perimeter, houses were burning, buildings were gutted or had collapsed and positions were being overrun. On each side of the bridge, the few remaining strongholds were subjected to heavy fire and blown apart. Yet, in spite of the deteriorating situation, Frost's men fought on. However, as the Germans reduced the last defences to smouldering rubble and Frost was badly injured by a mortar, almost 200 paratroopers finally emerged from their bombed and blasted positions and were prepared to finally accept capitulation.

As word was passed to Brinkmann that the bridge had been captured just before midday on 21 September, his *Kampfgruppe* began to finally remove the wreckage of Graebner's failed attack. Resistance was not totally suppressed and scattered fighting continued until mopping-up operations were completed by 23 September. Both sides appeared to be relieved it was all over.

Marching along as 2 Para's prisoner escort, Rudolf Trapp took the exhausted British prisoners past Knaust's resting column, which was reinforced and ready to move across the bridge to Elst. Private Sims remembers vividly the scene as he and his comrades turned into a road:

> Parked nose-to-tail were never-ending lines of German Mark IV tanks. In the dusk it was a truly impressive sight. A young German soldier called out, 'Yes Tommy, these were for you in the morning if you had not surrendered.' A number of SS tank men called out to us: 'Well fought, Tommy', 'Good fight, eh, Tommy.' They seemed to regard war in much the same way as the British regarded football.

With the capture of the Arnhem bridge, the focus of German activity shifted towards Nijmegen and west of Arnhem in Oosterbeek. The village of Oosterbeek itself had suffered terrible damage. For days it was pounded into rubble as SS troopers tried desperately to deny the British an exit west following their failed assault on the Arnhem bridge. In this ravaged landscape, which the SS were now calling *Der Hexenkessel* (the Witch's Cauldron), both sides fought bitterly. However, the situation was so desperate for the British that there was only one way out of the cauldron before being completely annihilated, which was to withdraw across the 400 yards of the Rhine to Driel.

A 2cm FlaK 38 gun crew with its Sd.Ah.51 trailer. The photograph was taken at Kastanjelaan at the junction where it crosses Boulevard Heuvelink and Johan de Wittlaan.

A portrait photograph of *SS-Hauptsturmführer* Hans Moeller. Moeller was commander of an engineer battalion: Pioneer Battalion 9. The unit comprised some eighty to ninety engineers with flame-throwers and a number of heavy machine guns. For several days the unit together with *Kampfgruppe Gropp* was heavily embroiled in fighting in the Arnhem area where it saw intense house-to-house battles. However, Moeller held his defence line along with Spindler's *Kampfgruppe* and eventually ground down the British paratroopers in a battle of attrition.

An SS soldier can be seen inside Arnhem in a residential area armed with his 98k Karabiner bolt-action rifle.

Panzergrenadiers can be seen along a road in Utrechtseweg. Note the destroyed 2cm FlaK 38 and the Sd.Anh.51 carrier.

British belongings are spread out along a road in Utrechtseweg. Methodically the Germans ground down the British. With ammunition and supplies fast running out in a number of areas, wholesale surrenders began taking place.

Two photographs showing British PoWs passing a stationary *Sturmgeschütz* belonging to Assault Gun 280. This photograph was taken on 20 September in Noorderweg, east of Oosterbeek. Both sides observed a short cease-fire that day, and these Paras have come from the emergency hospitals and are on their way to Arnhem.

Being escorted along a road, soldiers from the 1st Parachute Regiment have been taken prisoner.

SS-Brigadeführer Heinz Harmel confers with the commander, Stanislaw Sosabowski, of the 1st Independent Polish Parachute Brigade following its capture. During the operation, the brigade supported the British paratroopers at Oosterbeek. However, during the intense fighting that ensued, by 26 September the brigade had lost 25 per cent of its fighting strength, amounting to 590 casualties. To avert more casualties, it reluctantly surrendered.

Following being tended at a dressing station, these British Paras are questioned and searched by their captors at the side of a road.

British paratroopers being led away into captivity. They were totally exhausted, but both sides were relieved that the fighting was over.

British paratroopers raise their hands in surrender. *SS-Rottenführer* Rudolf Trapp was one soldier that escorted 2 Para prisoners along the Rijnkade. He said that the prisoners were for the most part bloody and bandaged with a few soldiers' pockets full of medical and other supplies.

SS soldiers round up a group of paratroopers which had been waiting for their captors. The failure to secure Arnhem was not the fault of the airborne forces which had held out tenaciously far longer than expected, but the operation as a whole.

Lieutenant Jack Reynolds of the 1st Airborne gives the two fingers to the camera in an act of defiance towards the Germans. Reynolds was later to say that 'I was so angry at the loss of fine young men and the carnage. Down the road I saw a German chap with a camera and a huge grin on his face and I thought what a bastard and gave him the opposite 'V' sign.'

A burned-out vehicle has been removed from the side of the road together with rubble and other pieces of debris following the Battle of Arnhem.

A photo taken at the end of the battle showing a knocked-out Pz.Kpfw.IV Ausf.G which was put out of action on 19 September. This tank belonged to the Mielke Company, which lost most of its armour trying to enter Arnhem.

A Pz.Kpfw.IV Ausf.H under a collapsed bridge in Westervoortsedjk which was part of the Mielke Company. The tank was probably lost either on 19 or 20 September.

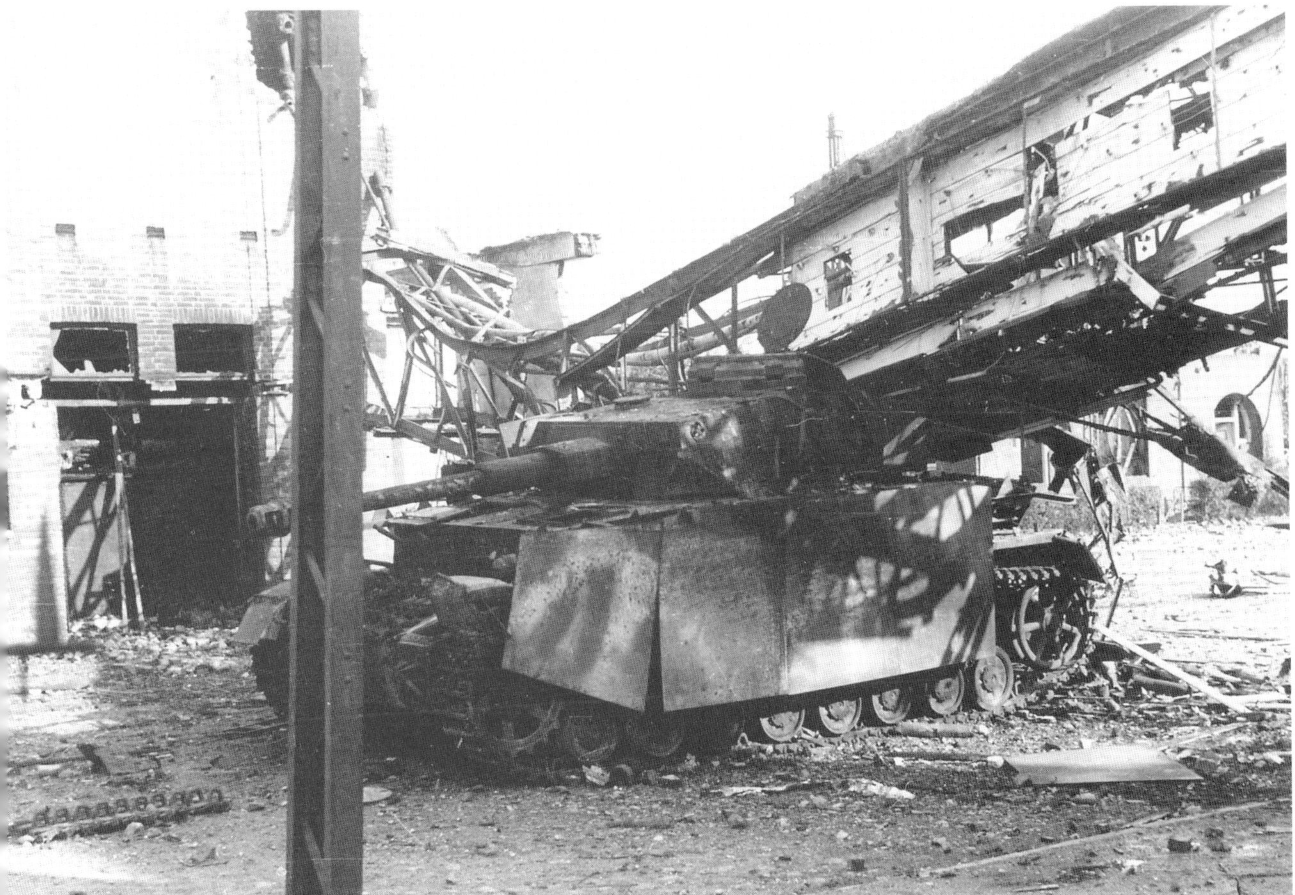

Epilogue

Some 10,000 men had dropped into Arnhem; some 2,000 made the crossing of the river. They left behind almost 300 wounded to be captured. Almost 3,000 were already in casualty stations; more than 1,200 British troops were dead. More than 3,400 German soldiers had been killed. The action lasted nine days. Though the SS battle at Arnhem together with its supporting Wehrmacht and *Fallschirmjäger* reinforcements was a temporary victory, as soon as the battle had ended *Hohenstaufen*, which had suffered since fighting in Holland started, was no longer capable of offensive action. For this reason it was immediately removed and departed from the area in order for its long-awaited rest and refit in the Reich. Regarding *Frundsberg*, it too had suffered high casualty rates but was compelled to contest XXX Corps' advance. Other remaining German forces in the region did not stop the fighting either. *Hauptsturmführer* Oelkers' *Kampfgruppe*, for instance, was ordered to form a bridgehead south of Arnhem over the Rhine and hold positions there until a continuous defence line had been established before it attacked. Supporting Oelkers' *truppen* was a motley collection of soldiers comprising naval personnel, men from the Hermann Göring Training Regiment and a Luftwaffe company. The force formed part of the II SS Panzer Korps offensive, which was a planned attack between the lower Rhine and Waal. In addition to these units, more troops arrived in the battle area which consisted of the 9th and 116th Panzer Divisions' *Kampfgruppen*. Supporting these ad hoc units was *Frundsberg*. Opposing them were strong British forces and later paratroopers from the 101st (US) Airborne Division.

For the attack, German units planned to cross the Rhine by Kasteel Doorwerth about 2,000 metres south-west of the Driel ferry. However, there were only a handful of boats for the offensive and the operation was a catastrophic failure. It was so bad that some SS men, in order to reach the far bank, were seen swimming part of the river, only to be immediately embroiled in hand-to-hand combat on arrival. Many soldiers were killed while crossing the river. Those that reached the far bank under a murderous gauntlet of fire found that they had nowhere to go. SS troops did manage to capture a brickworks factory, but the situation for the Germans had already deteriorated. For days with no resupply and ammunition running out, the bridgehead was ordered to be cleared out and those that could return back over the river were instructed to do so. Under the leadership of Oelkers' command, the withdrawal operation was a success.

Although the counter-attack across the Rhine had been successfully repulsed by the Allies, the front line in Holland would not move now until after the winter. However, the bridgeheads across the Maas and Waal still served as an important base for subsequent operations against the Germans on the Rhine, but this was constantly thwarted due to logistical problems and the winter fast closing in along the front.

This delay gave Hitler the opportunity to rebuild his army's strength in the west. The German army in the west was able to accumulate a strength of around 500 tanks and assault guns by early October, despite prioritizing new armour for operations on the Eastern Front. At the same time there was a huge German recruitment effort targeting German males between the ages of 16 and 60 to replace troops lost during the past five months of fighting on the Western Front. Premier Waffen-SS divisions were also replenished and strengthened.

As their strength grew, Wehrmacht forces began to reorganize themselves along a defensive front known as the Siegfried Line. Unbeknown to the Allies, these forces were not just moved into the area to perform defensive actions but would be part of a larger force that would undertake an offensive against Allied forces positioned in the Ardennes. This was the beginning of the build-up for what became known as the Ardennes offensive.

Following the failed Allied airborne landings in the Arnhem area any plans of successfully moving across the Rhine and into the Reich were thwarted. Yet, in spite of this failure, there was some bloody action in the south of Holland following the Battle of Arnhem including what was known as the Peel sector and the lower Rhine and Waal. Here German infantry are being moved towards the Rhine in October 1944.

Soldiers armed with the *Panzerfaust* in October 1944. These grenadiers were part of *Oelkers' truppen* which comprised a motley collection of men including naval personnel, infantry from the Hermann Göring Training Regiment and a Luftwaffe company. The force formed part of the II SS Panzer Korps' offensive which was a planned attack between the Lower Rhine and Waal.

Winter-clad grenadiers can be seen inside a wooded area during operations in the Lower Rhine area. These soldiers are part of the II SS Panzer Korps.

British troops being supported by armour advance through a village near the Rhine that has received extensive bomb damage. What remained of the II SS Panzer Korps withdrew behind the Rhine to begin a fanatical defence.

Appendix I

Order of Battle September 1944 (Holland)

Army Group B

Commanded by General Field Marshal Walther Model

II SS Panzer Korps

SS-Obergruppenführer Wilhelm Bittrich

9.SS Panzer Division *Hohenstaufen*: *SS-Obersturmbannführer* Walter Harzer

9.SS Panzer Regiment
19.SS Panzergrenadier Regiment
20.SS Panzergrenadier Regiment
9.SS Artillery Regiment
9.SS Aufk Battalion
9.SS PaK Battalion
9.SS Engineer Battalion
9.SS FlaK Battalion
9th SS Signals Battalion

10.SS Panzer Division *Frundsberg*: *SS-Brigadeführer* Heinz Harmel

10.SS Panzer Regiment
21.SS Panzergrenadier Regiment
22.SS Panzergrenadier Regiment
10.SS Artillery Regiment
10.SS Recon Battalion
10.SS PaK Battalion
10.SS Engineer Battalion
10.SS FlaK Battalion
10.SS Signals Battalion

Training Regiment of *Fallschirm*-Panzer Division 1: Hermann Göring, *Oberstleutnant* Fritz Fullriede

Kampfgruppe von Tettau: *Generalleutnant* Hans von Tettau

Kampfgruppe Krafft: *SS-Sturmbannführer* Sepp Krafft of Training and Replacement Battalion 16

Kampfgruppe Henke

15.Armee

General Gustav Adolf von Zangen

LXVIII Korps

General Otto Sponheimer

346.Infantry Division: General Erich Diestel

711.Static Division: General Josef Reichert
719.Coastal Division: General Karl Sievers

LXXXVIII Korps

General Hans-Wolfgang Reinhard
Kampfgruppe Chill: General Kurt Chill
59.Infantry Division: General Walter Poppe
245.Infantry Division: *Oberst* Gerhard Kegler
712.Static Division: General Friedrich-Wilhelm Neumann

LXXXVI Korps

General Hans von Obstfelder
176.Infantry Division: *Oberst* Christian Landau
Kampfgruppe Walther
6.*Fallschirmjäger* Regiment: *Oberst* Friedrich August Freiherr von der Heydte
107.Panzer Brigade: Major Freiherr von Maltzahn
Division *Erdmann*: General Wolfgang Erdmann

XII SS Korps

SS-Obergruppenführer Kurt von Gottberg
180.Infantry Division: General Bernhard Klosterkemper
190.Infantry Division: General Ernst Hammer
363. *Volksgrenadier* Division: General Augustus Dettling

Wehrkreis VI

Korps *Feldt*: General Kurt Feldt
406.*Landesschützen* Division: General Scherbenning

Luftwaffe West

Colonel General Kurt Student
1.*Fallschirmtruppen Armee*
I.*Fallschirmtruppen Korps*
II.*Fallschirmtruppen Korps*: General Eugen Meindl
86. *Korps*

Appendix II

Composition of a Waffen-SS and Wehrmacht Infantry and Panzergrenadier Division, 1944

Infantry Division, 1944

By the summer of 1944 both the Wehrmacht and the Waffen-SS infantry divisions had gone through a series of changes and had been modified and reorganized. The reconnaissance battalion, for instance, was removed and replaced with a bicycle-mounted reconnaissance platoon within every regiment. The anti-tank battalion was more or less made motorized and consisted of an anti-tank company equipped with *Jagdpanzer* IVs, *Hetzers* or StuGs, which were organized into three platoons of four vehicles and an HQ section of two vehicles, a motorized anti-tank company of twelve 7.5cm PaK 40 guns and a motorized FlaK company equipped with twelve 2cm or 3.7cm FlaK guns. The engineer battalion also took over the responsibility of the heavy weapons company. It comprised three engineer companies, each equipped with two 81cm mortars, two MGs and six portable flame-throwers. The heavy weapons in the engineer battalion were normally mounted in trucks, but by 1944 they were predominately pulled by draught animals, while the troops would be mounted on bicycles.

At regimental level an anti-tank company was added. This consisted of a platoon equipped with three 5cm PaK 38 guns and two platoons armed with *Panzerfausts*. Within the regiments, the infantry battalions were reduced in number to just two. A number of divisions in the field were attached with fusilier battalions and were structured identically to the new standard rifle battalion. The infantry battalions were equipped with four 12cm heavy mortars, while the rifle company's heavy weapons platoon was equipped with two 8.1cm mortars.

Panzer and Panzergrenadier Brigade, July 1944

By early July 1944 as the situation on the Western Front deteriorated Hitler outlined that his forces needed small, mobile, fast, armoured *Kampfgruppen* (fighting groups), which could be used effectively in action to meet the attacking enemy armoured formations. During the first week of July plans were issued to create these special armoured *Kampfgruppen*. They were to consist of at least one SPW-Battalion, one Panzer group with some forty Panzers, one PaK company and a number of FlaK wagons. In total about twelve such *Kampfgruppen*, named as Panzer Brigades, were to be issued to fighting units on the Eastern Front.

On 11 July the *Oberkommando des Heeres* (OKH) issued orders to create ten Panzer Brigades and these were designated as Panzer-Brigade 101 to 110. Each Panzer Brigade had one *Panzer-Abteilung* with three Panther companies, one *Panzerjäger* Company and one Panzergrenadier Battalion with four companies.

The Panzergrenadier Division 1944

By 1944 many infantry divisions were redesignated as Panzergrenadier divisions. Although having an armoured designation, the Panzergrenadier division was still technically an infantry formation. However, unlike a normal infantry division, there was a higher than usual attachment of armoured vehicles. A typical Panzergrenadier division had at least one battalion of infantry that were transported to the forward edge of the battlefield by Sd.Kfz.251 half-tracks and various armoured support provided by its own StuG Battalion. A typical Panzergrenadier division normally comprised an HQ company, a motorized engineer battalion and two Panzergrenadier regiments. Invariably a Panzergrenadier division had a StuG Battalion which contained an HQ Platoon equipped with three StuGs and three StuG companies. The StuG battalions were normally supported by a company comprising a StuG platoon which was equipped with four StuGs with 10.5cm guns, a FlaK platoon with three quad 2cm guns mounted on Sd.Kfz.6 or 7 half-tracks, an armoured engineer platoon with five Sd.Kfz.250 half-tracks and a motorized signal platoon.